KOHTA CIRCUS

KOHTA CIRCUS

A few more poems by

JOHN SCOTT BRINKERHOFF

proving
press

Book Design & Production:
Columbus Publishing Lab
www.ColumbusPublishingLab.com

Paperback ISBN: 978-1-63337-505-5

Printed in the United States of America
1 3 5 7 9 10 8 6 4 2

Cover Photo Credit: Dan Battagin
adventuretaco.com/kohta-circus   ·

For Larry Harris: Among the many words of our writers' craft, I could find none to describe how much your support in the last few years has meant to me. Thank you.

CONTENTS

Expatriate

This is an interesting place to which I've come,
one of human shapes that abruptly come and go,
splashes of light embedded in shadows,
and landscapes littered with fragments of artifacts
requiring a short period of study before being named.

Everyone here wears a veil with the opacity of morning fog,
therefore voices, height, hair and clothing are my only means
of distinguishing one from another.
They speak a different language than the one I know,
and my translations are often unreliable,
rendering my responses either comical or confusing.

Most people are affectionate and kind however,
forgiving my foreign ways.

I have been blessed with good weather and fine neighbors.
but have been here too long.
There are no sights left to see, few surprises left to delight.
There is an aimlessness to the hours.

Every day I go to the station, and then to the ticket agent,
who is no doubt weary of seeing me there,
and every day I ask, "When is the next train?"
The answer is always the same: "I don't know."

There is no point in getting all worked up about it,
because it is no less than I expect to hear.
"Why do you want to leave?" people have asked.

"Why are you willing to leave all this behind?"

I shrug. "Just tired of being a stranger, I suppose."

So I return to my rooms, so defined and familiar
I can easily navigate them in the dark,
and sit in my comfortable chair in a pool of light
with a book in hand and a dog at my feet,
to await what tomorrow brings.

ARRHYTHMIA

For two hours
this heart stumbled and staggered
in agitated confusion,
beating on the bars of my chest,
reaching up into my neck
      seeming to seek a way out.

It was given to me a long time ago
to counsel and care for,
which I have done dutifully,
if not always responsibly.
I have recklessly mislaid it on occasion,
or not shared it freely enough with those in need.
In my own defense, however,
I have also presented it
with times of surpassing joy, passion,
      and righteous purpose.

But this heart struggled for a while the other night
under the accumulated weight of age, red wine,
and intervals of indifference or despair.
Even so, it was not yet ready to quit,
laboring instead, I like to think, to turn around
from where we find ourselves right now,
fumbling to find a way for the two of us
to begin again—not start over, mind you,
because we lack the courage for that—
but content simply to go back
      the way we came.

DIASPORA

Everywhere, everywhere,
solemn multitudes breach the borders,
filling streets and parks and open doors,
overwhelming compassion where it lives
and upsetting the locals

They are the exiles driven from rubble,
cratered neighborhoods, nameless prisons,
the wrong religions or ancestral blood,
desiccated plains where only misery grows.
But all roads lead to Eden.

They've been here before, but never so many
and there is accusation in such numbers,
as if the groomed, orderly world owes them something
for all its failed attempts at salvation
and more successful attempts at plunder.

No one seems to understand that there are rules,
right ways and wrong ways to do things.
Founding principles are being challenged.
Unwritten laws of conduct are being ignored.
They cannot conform, but will not leave.

Shielding their children, clutching shapeless bundles,
they file by. Dark eyes in the dust reflect
the fear and suspicion they see looking back,
all along the way, as they pass,
shuffling into Babylon to conquer the kings.

Empty Church

A final chorus of gratitude releases us
from this holy human house.
Confessions have been murmured
and our transgressions forgiven
by a gentle hand that parted the air,
down and up, across and back again,
washing the dead.
Peace was passed from palm to palm,
soft hugs and smiles exchanged.
There are no more songs to sing,
and so the last long organ tones go forth alone.

Eddies of conversation form alongside
a leisurely outflow of parishioners, before they too
recede, leaving silence in the nave.
I stay for a while in the dignified refuge
below slender, particolored windows
 because I enjoy the emptiness.
The pews, in their rigid orderliness,
seem expectant, but also profoundly patient.
The altar and twin wooden sentinels,
each dressed in stately paraments,
present the promise of important arrivals.

A solitary figure hobbles into view and waves
before turning to tidy up the sanctuary
by making slow trips out of sight with tiny bundles,
and scratching here and there with a whisk broom.
Soon we will return to the wilderness outside

with its cold breath and broken clouds
where we will distractedly trudge along
under our burdens of mortal frailty and failure,
and offer sacrifices, real or symbolic,
to the greatest hope we have
as the only creature that fears for its soul.

KOHTA CIRCUS: THE ARTIST

In the shade of morning or afternoon
on a day before days, at an hour before hours,
an artist faces this canyon wall
and with fingertips and supple stick
leaves a new story or dream or only a sign
that joins a marvelous menagerie
of tumbling, trooping, flying figures
other artists left behind.
The artist is small
and concentrates on the work
of restoring life as a likeness
with fire ash and red dirt and drippings.

Perhaps the artist pauses for a moment,
shivers, and then quickly turns,
feeling the sudden chill of passing spirits
as we file behind him with our cameras
and floppy-brimmed hats and sunglasses,
peering over his shoulder before moving along.
The artist sends hasty prayers to the gods of ghosts
for protection, forgiveness, mercy.
The desert warmth returns.
The artist, now with another tale to tell,
completes his lines and leaves the busy stone
for numberless nights and days to consecrate,
to make all the still creatures of earth and water and air
holy again.

Weather Alert

I walked to a hilltop in my snowshoes,
to get away from everyone,
troubled by unhappy turns in my life,
and unmindful of a future foretold.

A snowfall began, with soft flakes
drifting leisurely down like feathers
through an absolute absence of wind.
As if witnessing the performance of a miracle,
I watched the dark smudges of houses below
submerge from sight.

When I turned back the way I had come,
the teardrop shapes of my tracks
had already been erased. There was no trace of me.
None.
I could have been dropped to this place from the sky
like the snow itself.

All around was utter stillness,
as it was long before then,
and will be long after now,
with the same question clearly asked
from the silence of my disappearing world.

> *Yes,* I answer.
> *I remember.*

REDUX

I see it over and over.

Watching our children play games in the grass,
I smelled the scents stirred up by their skipping feet,
and felt their joy in my chest, because I was only once removed
     from that lawn.

I sensed these things again when the grandchildren romped and ran,
while my own children remembered themselves for the first time.
I saw it in their eyes. Back and forth, back and forth.
     Tidal pulls of memory.

I see it in the trees as the sun retreats and returns—
brittle, bony limbs burdened with knotted buds
transform into rustling towers of shelter and peace.
     Gifts from winter's hand.

I see it over and over when darkness bows down to the horizon
where it waits to be dismissed by dawn. Waves, seasons,
even our own past show us how it is—sleep only passes through
     where light abides.

In A Crowd on a Sunny Afternoon

Trays banked with pinpoints of vivid color
as tightly nested as sunflower seeds
embrace the playing field.
How many? Five thousand? Ten? More?
But counting doesn't matter—
every soul is here for happiness.

Look closer and you see fathers and their kids,
old friends, new friends, boyfriends and girlfriends,
neatly overdressed business guests,
an old fellow, perhaps there for one more game
with his good-hearted son, smiling serenely
as he recalls the time The Mick stopped and said hello.

The rows are peppered with team colors on hats and shirts.
Early on, people traipse up and down wide-stepped aisles
carrying giant plastic cups and boxes or plates of food,
which will be balanced on their laps before ending up
under the seat for cleaning crews to clear away.
And then a contented idleness assimilates the sunlight.

But there are sudden, small whirlpools of motion
when the TV camera stops to stare
as two young women clap hands and sway like hula dancers,
or young men abruptly leap up, arms outstretched,
to snare a ball that arcs into their midst. One will hold it high,
triumphant, before they all settle back into their seats.

The home boys score; the crowd rises in a storm of sound—
applause, high fives, every voice soars, and every face smiles.
Whether or not we ever remember them,
we have these moments. We will always have these moments—
no matter what new joys may arrive,
or what horrors patiently wait.

FINDERS KEEPERS

Someone
throws a life away,
believing it dull,
meaningless,
and will never ever
be anything more.

Someone else,
always looking for treasure,
sees it glinting
from the grass—
"Look at this!
Look what I found!"

And clutching it tightly
so it won't slip away,
takes it home
to behold
from time to time,
with a satisfied smile,

thinking it
a wondrous thing,
a beautiful thing,
and so mysterious
in all the different ways
it shines in the light.

KINGS

There is no voice but our own in the murderous wind.
There is no comfort to be found in the shuddering earth.
There is no salvation in racing walls of flame.

All the answers are in the ineffable silence that follows.

Who will keep the journal of the end of our world?
Who will read it?

Mass Transit

Our clattering cradle rocks we few
into cocoons of indifference.
Eyes lock onto middle distance,
or a newspaper, or stare through grimy glass
at a swift stream of houses sketched in black and gray
that grow closer together and deeper into despair
against the dam of the city.

Fans of trash down the hillside point back at them,
summoning dread, demanding thanksgiving,
arousing vows of a more charitable heart.
There are flickers among us, brief looks up
to identify threat or inspiration for daydreams—
if glances collide, they ignite a humorless smile,
and quick return to impassiveness.

We hoard our countless lives to keep them safe
from discovery and theft, while creation continues
with every image, scent, thought, word, touch—
each infusing the others with illimitable change.
I will never know the trail of their strengths and frailties;
they will never know mine.
All we have in common is uniqueness.

And then we are assaulted by darkness and clamor.
Tunnel walls amplify the curious recitation
of steel wheels on rails: mypapa, mypapa, mypapa.
Shrieks, jolts, a descending hum as we slow to a stop.
Outside now, in sick, underground light, are milling shapes,
numberless lives hurrying to their destinies. The doors open wide.
We step into infinity.

JOHN SCOTT BRINKERHOFF

THE POND IN SPRING

One morning, unannounced, the ducks are there,
treading through water the ice left behind.
The geese come days later, homeward bound,
to rest and nest in their big floating baskets
   near the cattails.

The gander barks furiously as it flies overhead.
His long neck, stretched out, becomes a harsh trumpet
loud enough to rouse all the bundled sleepers—
Wake up, he calls. *Wake up!*
It's time!

ON THE OTHER HAND

At an informal afternoon gathering of friends,
along with a few acquaintances with unusual appeal,
small stands of guests shifted and swayed like rushes
within a steady stream of conversation,
from which occasional bubbles of laughter rose,
and bottles, glasses, crockery and food warmers,
all nicely arranged, lined the banks,
someone partially inhaled a bite of lobster.

The victim turned out to be a mature lady
of independent means and mind, whose opinions
she shared with inarguable authority.
A woman close by noticed her sudden struggle,
animated by frantic gestures toward her throat,
and began slapping the lady on her back.
Others, alarmed by then, gathered around to watch
the unfortunate, wide-eyed lady slowly turn blue.

I rushed over without really thinking about it
to exercise a maneuver I had learned years ago
when learning the maneuver was popular.
I encircled her with my arms from behind,
a thumb knuckle aimed toward her solar plexus,
and gave her a sudden, hearty hug.
The lobster chunk was abruptly airborne.
She began dragging in lungsful of blessed air.

There was then a great deal of relief among all,
and my own was coupled with wonder

that the technique worked so well.
The party resumed its intended course.
Years later, while walking through a store,
I encountered her. She fondly patted my arm.
"Have I ever told you?" she said. "When you helped me?
You broke one of my ribs."

REFRAIN

Some day, I'm going to Italy.
Eat the food, drink the wine.
Walk the streets of mountain towns
and visit ruins.

Some day, I'm going to write a book.
Maybe it will be about my life,
Or maybe one about a life
I imagine.

Some day, I want to bungee jump
off a bridge, or some other high place,
just to see what it's like
to fall that far.

Some day, I'm going to make an effort
to find someone who needs help
and help them, and not even tell them
who I am.

Some day, I'll give the dog a bath,
and then take her for a good, long walk
while I talk to all the neighbors
I haven't seen in ages.

I swear I will some day,
before it's too late.

JOHN SCOTT BRINKERHOFF

CHICAGO, IN THE SPRING

For so many years we shared common ground—
the same rooms and windows,
the same lawns and coarse sand beaches,
school hallways and gymnasiums.
We bathed you in smiles and pride,
while you accumulated your achievements.
And yet, all along, your eyes and voice hinted
that they were merely lessons being gathered
      for some other purpose.

Looking back, we knew that common ground
was never for you. To some degree,
each of us has felt the same stirring,
when the unbound fields become confining,
the enduring familiarities become alien,
and open arms become too restrictive.
We know how talk can grow smaller and smaller
until there is little left to do but listen
      in wonder or sympathy.

Your opportunities, then, come as no surprise,
and your leave-taking bears signs of inevitability.
But we are also certain that you understand
how memory will not be suppressed,
nor our own lessons be unlearned
when we call out, "Farewell, good luck, Godspeed,"
as you, waving once before turning to face
the great, wide world ahead,
      go on your way.

BEDTIME STORY

Captain America
dives from the shower curtain rod
splash! into bath water.
Whoa! That was a good half-gainer..

Next goes The Hulk,
boulder muscles and all
splash!
I think he hit bottom on that one.

They float around
with other plastic toys
and just as still.
Okay, let's get you ready for bed.

A small body
Wrapped up tight
In a blue towel.
You look like a mummy. King Toot?

A dusting of powder
and then pjs,
the ones with elephants on them.
What? I sound like a pig? Well, you smell good.

Plop, against the pillow.
Covers pulled up and over
in low lamplight.
Name the story you want to hear.

Of course,
Bartholomew Cubbins. Again.
They even made some Ooblek once.
Sure, I'll lie down next to you.

  The life everlasting.
  World without end.
    Amen.

Alter Ego

We are the same,
but nothing alike.

When one shoves roughly forward,
the other is disappointed by his weakness.

One can be fierce and unforgiving,
the other, kind and embracing.

One can be rude and resentful,
the other, prayerful and obedient.

We don't know which is real,
and which is the practiced pretender.

Is one an author of wreckage,
or a guardian of righteousness?

Perhaps one exists to conceal the other,
or both are imagined as what each wishes to be.

No matter. In the end, a glorious transformation
will absolve one of us of his secrets.

while the other wanders in gloom, eyes cast down,
looking for a place to rest in Judas' field.

INVOCATION CHORUS

Let there be one person,
just one, before I go,

who looks upon me with utterly selfless pride
and unconcealed love.

One person who hears what I say
without challenge or mockery or disregard.

One person who sees past my skin or faith or features
into the glittering mine of my worth.

Just one person,
before I go,

who embraces for dear life,
and says, "Finally, finally,
           I have found you."

THE WORDS

We can search for the words all day long,
but the words will find us when they choose to—
        some arriving with a flash,
        others with a flutter.

The words do not create
our memories and imaginings,
but will reconstruct them,
one by one—
        No, this goes here,
        that goes there.

All we can do is catch them
like fireflies,
put them side by side in rows
and boxes
and little buildings,
        and know
        they will stay.

Some days, we may not recall them,
        but the words
        will never forget us.

AN UPPERMOST ROOM
(A Consideration of J. L. Dickey)

Every evening the poet ascends his mountain
from a base camp near the foyer.
He is alone and infirm now,
evidence of a successfully self-destructive nature.
He requires rich air for the climb
      and rest at every turn.

After gathering strength at the bottom of the slope,
the poet lugs his oxygen tank up the first step

then the next

and the next,

twelve in all

to the first landing.

His vision had by then tunneled inward,
daring a falter to show itself,
but he is released on level ground
to collapse onto a chair he has left there.

He pants for awhile as his enfeebled lungs
labor to repay their debt to his effort.
No one can suppose the proceedings
of the poet's mind, but certainly
reflection and study are at work

on recollections from a life of leaf-broken light,
darkness and brilliance inseparable,
that sought to dapple every cleft and mound and river and road
      under the sun;
not to conquer them, not to conquer—
but to extract the meaning of them,
which he refined with his own fire and poured out
as talismans and mythic totems
made of words.

     Onward.

Stubborn resolve prods him to his feet.
The poet plods to landing two
where he again bends himself into a waiting chair
for further introspection and recasting.
Perhaps a word or two or three will emerge
that demand to be remembered in the morning,
or perhaps he will discover that he has lost hope
     by finding regret among them.

He is near rooms—bedrooms, office, bathroom—
but the poet will not stop here.
He will move on, up one more flight, to the summit,
to a space below the roof.
     and a bed beneath a skylight.

In the company of books at attention on low shelves,
the poet rests his head on a pillow,
against a flimsy fan of long white hair.
His breathing slows as he contemplates the night sky,

closer here, above the obfuscation of trees,
where darkness and brilliance are inseparable,
       while,
with the compassionate embrace of motherhood,
all of spangled creation
       watches over him.

Between The Hours

I
The sun breaks.
The soldiers turn away
from the deep creases
wagon wheels have left in the mud
to return home.

They step and sway,
slowed by confusion,
trying to recall sleep
and the look of things
unbroken.

You can see that some
crawl into shade, and others
will themselves
into gray marches
up the pale, steep hills.

But they all stop,
looking for the source of a sound.
it's a new year's day,
and the trains
are running again.

II
I was born in 1944,
then curled, blanketed and blind, beneath smoke-stung eyes
that clutched the dear trees

before losing them in sliding glaze.
The rails clawed away her life, our life,
even though we were already far from there,
from a time of broad flowered hats and white gloves,
veiled faces, rippling blue dresses,
a smile and tender kiss,
a long-ago Missouri only hours old.
The serious girl on a golden lawn
waved goodbye
and went into the house.
The stolid, broad-backed river looked up once
and was gone.
How far have we come?
Not far, but too far to ever go back.
The cradle rocks all strangers alike,
and sings to them the same.
Look at the people.
They are hurt and homeless
and don't know why.
and all the way north
the rain billowed over the plains like sails
in 1944.

We arrived wearing the echoes
of tolling steel and huffing locomotives
in a springtime that grew colder by the hour,
and worked against an incoming tide
matted with flotsam from the war—
eyes, ears, noses gone from faces,
a crumpled stump of jaw,
ragged ridges of slick, pink skin,

a neatly pinned flag of shirtsleeve,
or half-empty pant leg folded up—
so many, so many,
And some turned to smile at me.

Black and white,
the smell of ether,
the weight of books
and the lightness of wasted hours.
awakening to the omens
of cigarette smoke in the air
and watery bourbon left in a glass,
running, running, running—
these things live in their moments like bellsong,
sharp when newly struck,
full as they fade away
leaving a sadness that hums in the heart.

Such is the meanness of memory,
which endures to mock us.
Where the recollection of close friends
only points to their empty places.
Or the remembrance of triumph
forces us to count our losses.
Even in its absence, memory refines
the arguments of our existence,
for how often do our hands
fly desperate to one another
to clutch the stems of prayer?
And how often do our measured steps to the door
become more grueling than to run?

Perhaps at the end
when we slip between the hours
we discover what it is we long for.
But each day until then, within my mirror,
the tricks of my own ruined sight
bring together the ends of my life,
for when I look into one eye the other is gone,
when I see one cheek, an ear has vanished,
or nose, or bearded jaw.
Do you see how memory works?
Perhaps the wounded knew when they smiled at me.
Perhaps they knew.
I smile back at them.

III
We cleave time
like waders in water,
in the same instant
embraced and released,
found and lost.

Change comes
In cold currents,
brought upon us
under a sheet of sunlight
that burns the eyes.

We become
strangers to the language,
and find ourselves
in a different country
without ever having moved.

Helpless, we transform
into our fathers, mothers,
and become their children again,
lifting bruised limbs
for a kiss.

But come some blue morning
we will falter and fall,
slip under,
and will at last be able to hear
the tumbling of the stars.

Also by the author:

All In Time

Dinosaurs

The Cloud Fisher